First Ride on a School Bus with Tamir

Whitney Sanderson

Lerner Publications ◆ Minneapolis

Discover six early milestones alongside your favorite *Sesame Street* friends! From visiting the dentist to getting a library card, this series helps young children feel prepared for new and exciting experiences that are a part of growing up.

Sincerely,
The Editors at Sesame Workshop

Table of Contents

Here Comes the Bus

There are lots of different ways to get to school. You might walk, ride your bike, ride in a car, or ride on the school bus.

I love riding the school bus to school! Last week I sat next to my friend Sam.

Riding to School

If you ride the bus, you'll learn where your bus stop is before the first day of school. This is a place you will go each day to meet the bus.

Granny Bird and I sing songs while we wait.

Your grown-up will walk with you to the bus stop and wait with you.

I always wave to my Papi before the bus drives away!

The bus driver will open the doors for you once they get to your stop. You can use stairs and a railing inside the bus to get on. People who use wheelchairs can go up a lift to board the bus.

The bus driver makes sure everyone gets to school safely.

You will probably have the same bus driver every day.

Once you're on the bus, you'll find your seat. Sometimes you can choose to sit with a friend or meet someone new.

Hi, I am Grover.
Can I sit with
you?

Once everyone is sitting down, the school bus will start moving. It will stop often to pick up other kids on the way to school.

I see my friend
Elmo waiting for
the bus!

It is important to stay in your seat until the bus gets to school. During your ride to school, you can talk with your friends!

Do you want to play together at recess, Elmo?
Yes! Elmo and Abby can play on the playground!

You can also play games like I spy. To play I spy, describe something you see, and a friend will guess what it is. Then it's their turn to describe something and your turn to guess.

I spy something blue.
Is it my lunch box?
Yes!

Once the school day is over, your bus will be waiting to bring you back home.

Riding the school bus is a great way to get to and from school!

School Bus Fun

Here are some things you can do on the school bus:

1. Talk to a friend.
2. Sing songs.
3. Read a book.
4. Say hi to someone new.
5. Play I spy or another game.

Glossary

bus stop: a place where people go to meet the school bus, usually near their home

driver: the person who starts, steers, and stops the school bus

lift: a part with a motor that helps people who use wheelchairs get on the school bus

railing: a long bar that people grab onto for safety

Read More

Bassier, Emma. *Bus Safety*. Minneapolis: Cody Koala, 2021.

Gabor, Nicole. *First Day of School with Ji-Young*. Minneapolis: Lerner Publications, 2026.

Pang, Ursula. *Buses*. Buffalo: PowerKids, 2025.

Photo Acknowledgments

Image credits: leekris/Getty Images, p. 3; kali9/Getty Images, p. 4; Kevin Lohka/Dreamstime, p. 7; SDI Productions/Getty Images,pp. 8, 18, 21; LightFieldStudios/Getty Images, p. 10; FG Trade Latin/Getty Images, p. 12; FatCamera/Getty Images, pp. 14, 16. Design element: Agunar/Shutterstock.

Cover: FatCamera/Getty Images.

Index

To Faisal

Lerner Publications Company
An imprint of Lerner Publishing Group, Inc.
241 First Avenue North
Minneapolis, MN 55401 USA

For reading levels and more information, look up this title at www.lernerbooks.com.

Main body text set in Mikado.
Typeface provided by HvD Fonts.

Designer: Mary Ross **Photo Editor:** Lucien Brinkley

Library of Congress Cataloging-in-Publication Data

Names: Sanderson, Whitney, author.
Title: First ride on a school bus with Tamir / Whitney Sanderson.
Description: Minneapolis : Lerner Publications, [2026] | Series: Sesame Street firsts | Includes bibliographical references and index. | Audience term: Children | Audience: Ages 4–8 | Audience: Grades K–1 | Summary: "Join Tamir and his friends from Sesame Street in riding on the bus for the first time. From waiting for the bus to the ride to school, readers will feel prepared for this milestone"— Provided by publisher.
Identifiers: LCCN 2024038563 (print) | LCCN 2024038564 (ebook) | ISBN 9798765661055 (library binding) | ISBN 9798765684832 (paperback) | ISBN 9798765680933 (epub)
Subjects: LCSH: Sesame Street (Television program)—Juvenile literature. | School buses—Juvenile literature. | School children—Transportation—Juvenile literature. | Ability in children—Juvenile literature. | Child development—Juvenile literature.
Classification: LCC LB2864 .S34 2026 (print) | LCC LB2864 (ebook) | DDC 371.8/72–dc23/eng/20241211

LC record available at https://lccn.loc.gov/2024038563
LC ebook record available at https://lccn.loc.gov/2024038564

Manufactured in the United States of America
1-1011810-53660-12/19/2024